11-4

Play & Sing-
It's Christmas!

Play & Sing-
It's Christmas!

A PIANO BOOK OF EASY-TO-PLAY CAROLS

Brooke Minarik Varnum

Illustrated by Emily Arnold McCully

MACMILLAN PUBLISHING CO., INC.
New York
COLLIER MACMILLAN PUBLISHERS
London

AUTHOR'S NOTE

When I began teaching piano, I didn't have access to many teaching materials. The method presented here evolved as dessert for students who wanted to play familiar songs. Since there's such a short season to play and sing Christmas carols, I worked out this method, which is uncomplicated by note and rhythmic notation. The introduction to the carols came about because I wanted to make this method available to those children who don't take piano lessons but may have a piano that they can use. These few pages contain only the information necessary to play the carols and, for very young children, may be understood with the help of a parent or friend.

For my mother

I wish to thank my teacher and friend Ruth S. Edwards, Associate Professor of Music at the University of New Hampshire, for her invaluable editorial assistance in the preparation of this book.

Library of Congress Cataloging in Publication Data
Main entry under title: Play & sing—it's Christmas!
Summary: Simple instructions teach the beginner to play 16 well-known Christmas carols on the piano. 1. Piano music, Juvenile. 2. Christmas music. 3. Carols. [1. Carols. 2. Christmas music] I. Varnum, Brooke Minarik. II. McCully, Emily Arnold.
M1378. P714   1980   [(M5200)]   783.6'552   80-15967   ISBN 0-02-791400-3

Contents

Introduction and instructions   6–21

CAROLS

Angels We Have Heard on High   42
Away in a Manger   28
Christmas Is Coming   40
Deck the Halls   46
God Rest You Merry, Gentlemen   38
Good King Wenceslas   30
Hark! the Herald Angels Sing   44
Jingle Bells   24
Jolly Old Saint Nicholas   47
Joy to the World!   29
O Come, All Ye Faithful   34
Over the River and Through the Woods   26
The First Nowell   36
Up on the House Top   32
We Three Kings of Orient Are   31
We Wish You a Merry Christmas   48

The old Christmas carols everyone knows so well
are fun to sing and to play on the piano.
If you enjoy Christmas carols
and want to play them on the piano,
this book will show you how to do just that—
even though you may have never studied piano
or have had only a few lessons.
Before you start playing the carols, though,
there are a few things you need to know.

To begin with, the piano keyboard
is made up of white keys and black keys.
Here's a drawing of part of the piano keyboard.

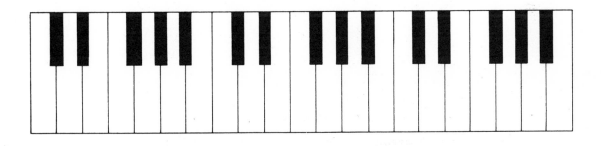

As you see, the white keys are one next to the other,
and the black keys are in groups of two or three.
To play the carols in this book,
you will need to use only the white keys.

When you play the piano from left to right,
you are playing up the keyboard.

———————————————> UP

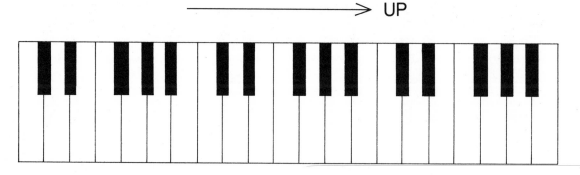

As you play up the keys, they sound higher.
Try playing all the white keys up the keyboard.
Don't worry now about which finger plays which key.

Playing from right to left is playing down the keyboard.

DOWN ⟵—————————————

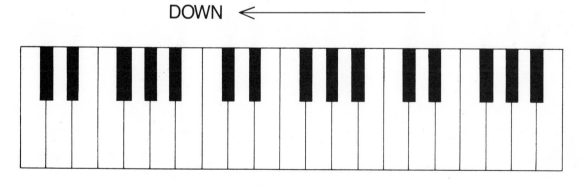

As you play down the keys, they sound lower.

Now try playing all the white keys down the keyboard.

The white keys are named by letters in the alphabet.
Seven letters, ABCDEFG, are used again and again.
ABCDEFG is called the musical alphabet.

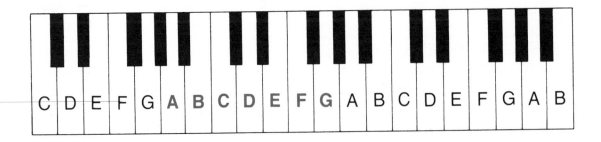

The alphabet is ABCDEFG going up the keyboard,
and GFEDCBA going down the keyboard.

Now you are ready to name and play the white keys.

In this book, you will start by naming A's because

A is the first letter in the musical alphabet.

A is in the group of three black keys.

Can you find and play all the A's

up and down the keyboard?

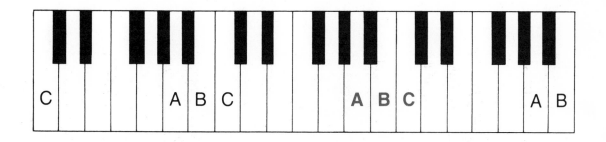

B and C are the next white keys up from A.

Try playing and naming groups of ABC up the keyboard

and groups of CBA down the keyboard.

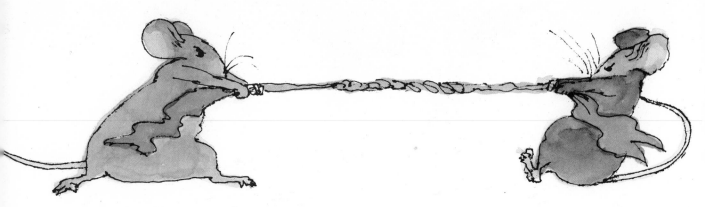

Two more white keys are D and E.

Play and name groups of CDE up the keyboard

and EDC down the keyboard.

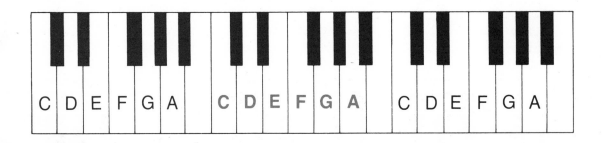

And finally, the last two letters are F and G,

the next white keys up from E.

The white key up from G is A—

and the musical alphabet starts all over again.

You can now play and name groups of EFGA up the keyboard

and AGFE down the keyboard.

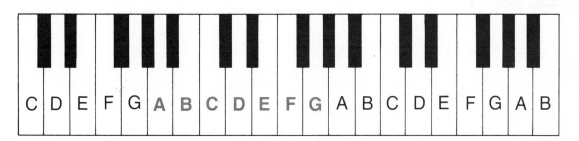

Now put it all together by playing and naming
ABCDEFG up and GFEDCBA down the keyboard.
You can now name and play all of the white keys
on the piano. Try it and see.

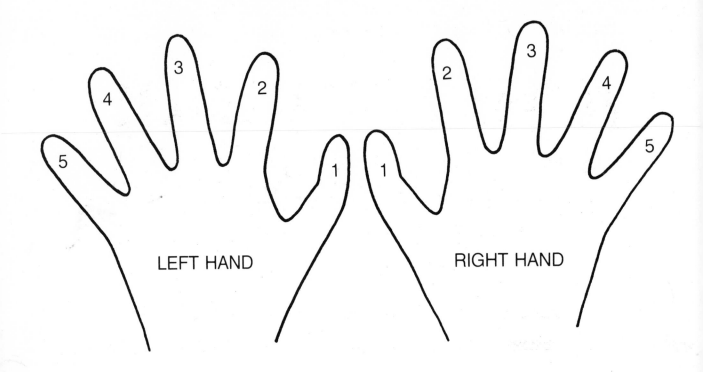

LEFT HAND   RIGHT HAND

When playing the piano, your fingers have numbers
so that it's easy to keep track of which finger
goes on which key.
Hold out your hands and wiggle your fingers
as you call out their numbers.
Your thumbs are 1.
Your fingers next to your thumbs are 2,
and so on down to your little finger which is 5.
To play the carols in this book,
you will always use both hands.

Now, put your fingers on these keys.

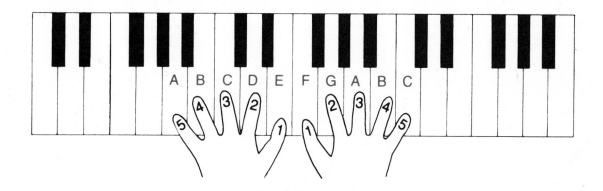

Then, play and name up the keyboard ABCDEFGABC.

And then play and name down the keyboard CBAGFEDCBA.

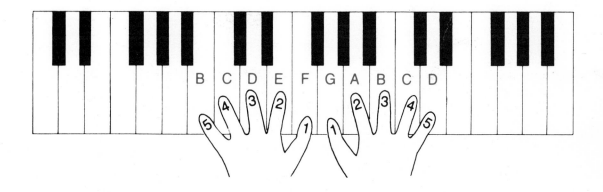

Try some different notes. Play and name BCDEFGABCD up
and DCBAGFEDCB down the keyboard.
To learn the names of the white keys really well,
it is best to do the same thing beginning on C,
then D, then E, then F, and then G.

Here are some things to keep in mind.

In some carols, you'll repeat keys like this—E E E:

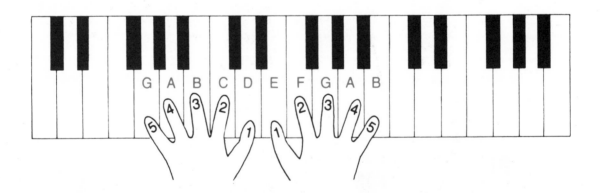

With all your fingers on the keyboard,

play E with your right hand (1) three times.

Or, you'll play keys one next to the other like this—C D E:

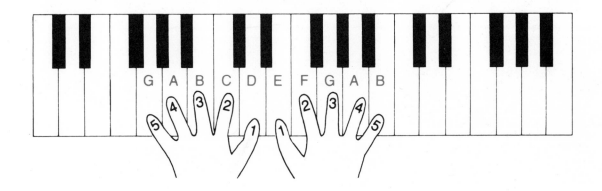

Both hands play here.

Your left hand plays C and D, and your right hand plays E.

Sometimes, you'll skip keys like this—G C E:

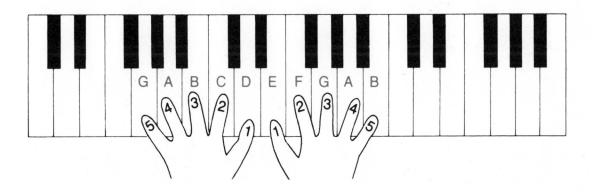

Again, both hands play. Your left hand plays G and C,

and your right hand plays E.

If this is a little tricky,

why not try it more than once?

Each carol will have a drawing of part
of the piano keyboard. The drawing will show you
exactly where to put your fingers on the keys.
"Jingle Bells" will have this drawing, so to play it,
you put your fingers over these keys.

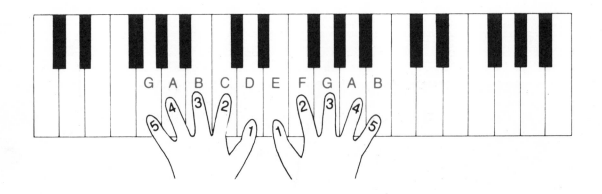

The words to each of the carols are written out like this:

```
E  E  E     E  E  E
```
Jingle bells! Jingle bells!

```
E  G        E
```
Jingle all the way.
```
       C  D
```

The letters above the words name keys
that are to be played with your right hand.
And the letters below the words name keys
that are to be played with your left hand.
Now try singing and playing the first
two lines of "Jingle Bells."

You may play any of these carols anywhere on the keyboard,

on high or low keys.

But the keys nearest the middle of the piano

are the easiest to sing with.

If you can sing the carols, you can play them.

It's fun to sing along while you play,

and others can sing with you.

Don't worry if you don't know one of the carols.

Just let someone sing it for you first

to give you an idea of how it goes.

The main thing is to have fun singing and playing.
Especially playing.
And the nicest part is that when you play,
people will sing—
even if you make a few mistakes.
So, happy caroling! And Merry Christmas!

The Carols

JINGLE BELLS

```
 E   E      E   E
Jingle Bells!   Jingle Bells!
```

```
 E  G       E
Jingle all the way.
       C  D
```

```
 F   F   F F E  E
Oh, what fun it is to ride
```

```
 E  E      E       G
In a one horse open sleigh—hey!
       D    D     D
```

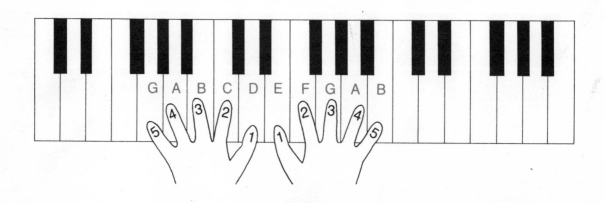

E E E   E E E
Jingle Bells!   Jingle Bells!

E G   E
Jingle all the way.
     C D

F   F F F F E E
Oh, what fun it is to ride

E E G   G F
In a one horse open sleigh.
             D   C

25

OVER THE RIVER
AND THROUGH THE WOODS

G G G G   G   G   G

Over the river and through the woods,
           E F

G   C   C C   B A G

To Grandmother's house we go.

 G

The horse knows the way to carry the sleigh,
   F   F   F   F FEE E

                          G

Through deep and drifted snow—oh!
E   D   E   D   D

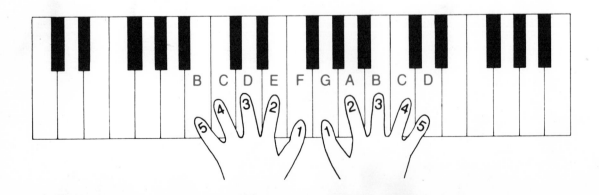

G G G G   G   G   G
Over the river and through the woods,

           E F

G C C B A G
Oh, how the wind does blow.

G C   C B A G C
It stings the toes and bites the nose,

                         E

  G G G
As over the ground we go.

F   F   D C

AWAY IN A MANGER

G GF E   E D
Away in a manger,

No crib for a bed,
C   C   B A G

                    D
The little Lord Jesus
G GA G   G

                         E
Laid down His sweet head.
B   A   G   C

G   G   F E E D
The stars in the sky

Looked down where He lay,
C   C   B A G

        FE   D   E D
The little Lord Jesus
G

        D
Asleep on the hay.
C   A B   C

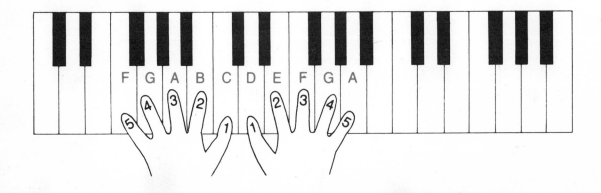

JOY TO THE WORLD!

C B A   G
Joy to the world! The Lord is come.
　　　　　　　F　E　D　C

G　A　A B　B　C
Let earth receive her King.

C CBAG G
Let every heart
　　　　F E

C C B AG G
Prepare Him room,
　　　F E

　　　　　　　　　G
And heaven and nature sing,
　E　　E　　E　E E F

And heaven and nature sing,
FE　　D　　D　DDE　F

　　　　C A G
And heaven and heaven
E D　C　　　　F E

And nature sing.
F　E D C

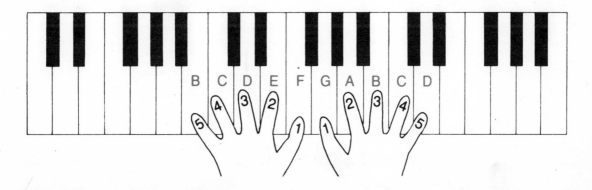

29

GOOD KING WENCESLAS

               D
Good King Wenceslas looked out
  C   C   C   C   C   G

On the feast of Stephen,
 A   G   A   B   C   C

              D
When the snow lay round about,
  C   C   C   C   C G

Deep and crisp and even.
  A   G   A   B C C

  G   F   E   D   E   D
Brightly shone the moon that night,
                       C

Through the frost was cruel,
  A   G   A   B   C C

                    D
When a poor man came in sight,
  G   G   A   B   C   C

  G   F   E D   F
Gathering winter fu—el.
            C   C

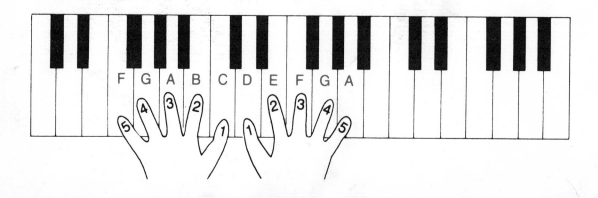

30

WE THREE KINGS OF ORIENT ARE

E   D
We three Kings of Orient are
            C   A BCB A

  E D
Bearing gifts we traverse afar,
          C   A   B   BA

         D D   E   E   GFE
Field and fountain, moor and mountain,
  C   C

D E D
Following yonder star.
         C B A

  D
Oh—star of wonder, star of light,
B   C C C G C A C

Star with royal beauty bright,
C   C   CG C A   C

       D E F   E D E
Westward leading, still proceeding,
  C   C

Guide us to thy perfect light.
C   C CG C A C

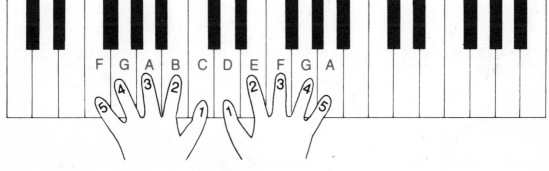

UP ON THE HOUSE TOP

G G A G   G

Up on the house top reindeer pause,

         E   C   E

A   A   G   G G

Out jumps dear old Santa Claus;

        E   D

G   G   A   G   G

Down through the chimney with lots of toys,

           E   E   C   E

A   A   A   GG   G

All for the little ones Christmas joys.

         E   D   C

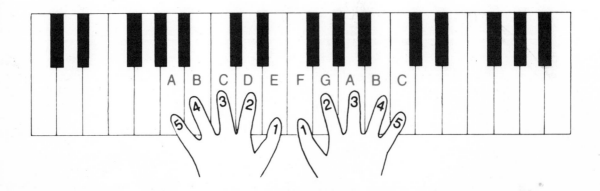

32

F F A G G
Ho, ho, ho! Who wouldn't go!
                                    E

        F   G G
Ho, ho, ho! Who wouldn't go—
D D   E   C E

G G A G   F G A
Up on the house top—click, click, click—
                            E

    G   G   A G   G
Down through the chimney with good Saint Nick.
                            E   E   D   C

O COME, ALL YE FAITHFUL

D
O come, all ye faithful,
C C   G C   G

E D E FE   D
Joyful and triumphant,

D E
O come ye, O come ye to Bethlehem.
C   C   B A B C   B A G G

G   F   E F   E
Come and behold Him,

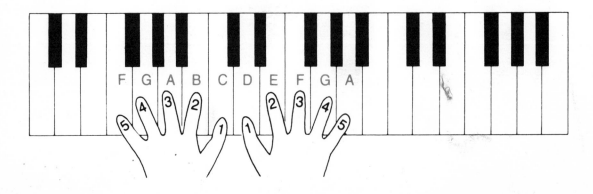

34

    D   E   D

Born the King of Angels.

                C   B A G

             D

O come, let us adore Him,

C   C   B   C   C   G

E   E   D E F E   D

O come, let us adore Him,

E F   E D   F

O come, let us adore Him,

                  C B C

  E D

Christ the Lord.

       C   C

THE FIRST NOWELL

G
The first Nowell,

E D CD EF

A B C B A G
The angel did say,

A B C B A G A
Was to certain poor shepherds

B C G
In fields as they lay.

F E

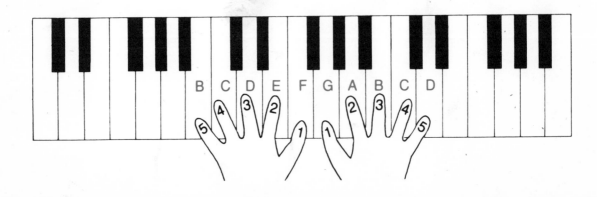

<pre>
                   G
In fields where they
ED CD   EF

AB C B   A G
Lay keeping their sheep,

  A B C   B A GA
On a cold winter's night

  B C G
That was so deep.
           F   E

               G CB A A   G
Now—ell, now—ell, now—ell, now—ell,
ED   CD EF

  C B A GA B CG
Born is the King of Is—ra—el.
                    F   E
</pre>

37

GOD REST YOU MERRY, GENTLEMEN

          E   E D
God rest you merry, gentlemen,
   A   A   C B A

              D   E
Let nothing you dismay.
  G A B C

          E   E   D
For Jesus Christ, our Saviour,
   A   A   C B A

               D   E
Was born on Christmas Day.
  G A B C

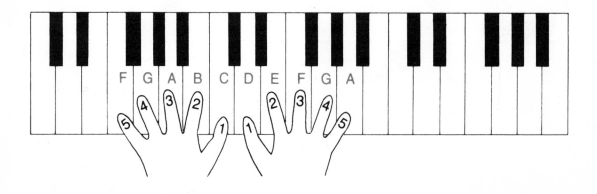

E F D E F   G A E
To save us all from Satan's power,

D   D
When we were gone astray.
       C A   B   C

   D E F   E ED
Oh—tidings of comfort and joy,
C   C B A

                    D
Comfort and joy,
   C B A

   D E F G   A E D
Oh—tidings of comfort and joy.
C   C B A

39

CHRISTMAS IS COMING

C C   B A A

Christmas is coming,

A   G   A G

The goose is getting fat.

F   E

G

Won't you please put a penny

E   F   C C D D

In the old man's hat?

F F E   D   .C

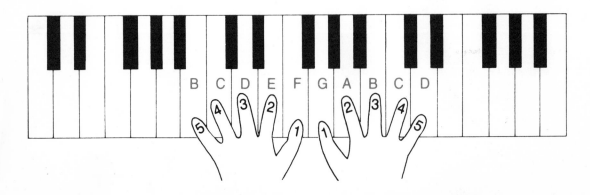

40

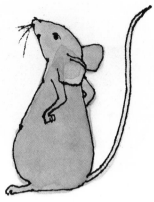

GG CC CBAA
If you haven't got a penny,

AG AG
A half penny will do.
        F E

      GG
If you haven't got a half penny,
E F   CCD   DF

God bless you!
   E   D   C

ANGELS WE HAVE HEARD ON HIGH

E E E G   G   F E
Angels we have heard on high,

E D E G   E D
Sweetly singing o'er the plains,
                    C

E   E   E G   G F E
And the mountains in reply,

E DE   G   E D
Echoing their glorious strains,
                    C

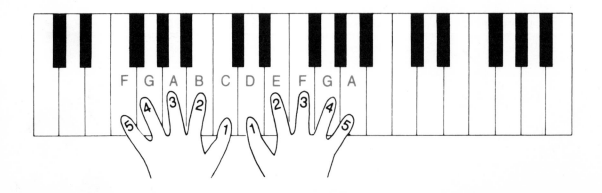

G AGFEF GFEDE FED D

Glo_____, _____, _____ria,
                                        C   GG

      D EF E D

In excelsis Deo!

C

G AGFEF GFEDE FED D

Glo_____, _____, _____ria,
                                            C   GG

      D EF   ED

In excelsis De—o!

C   C

HARK! THE HERALD ANGELS SING

          E ED

Hark! the herald angels sing,

  G C   CB C

  G G G F   E   D   E

"Glory to the newborn King!

                E   E

Peace on earth, and mercy mild,

 G   C   C   B   C   D

  G D D

God and sinners reconciled."

      C B A G

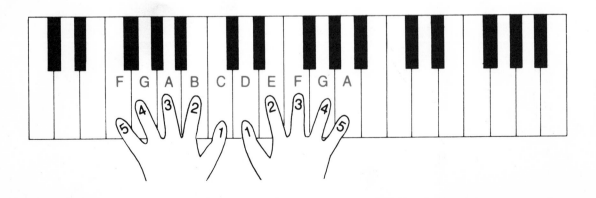

G   G   G   F E   ED
Joyful, all ye nations, rise,
          C

G   G   G   F E   ED
Join the triumph of the skies;
          C

A   A   AG   F   E   F
With th' angelic host proclaim,

D   EF G   D E
"Christ is born in Bethlehem!"
         C C

A   A   AG   F   E   F
Hark! the herald angels sing,

D   EF G   D
"Glory to the newborn King!"
        C C   C

DECK THE HALLS

G
Deck the halls with boughs of holly,
   F   E   D   C   D E C

Fa la la la la, la, la, la, la.
D E F D E D C B C

G
'Tis the season to be jolly,
   F   E D C D E C

Fa la la la la, la, la, la, la.
D E F D E D C B C

                   G
Don we now our gay apparel,
  D   E   F   D   E   F   D

    G A B C B A G
Fa la la, la la la, la, la, la.
E F

G
Troll the ancient Yuletide carol,
   F   E D   C D   E C

A A A A G
Fa la la la la, la, la, la, la.
       F E D C

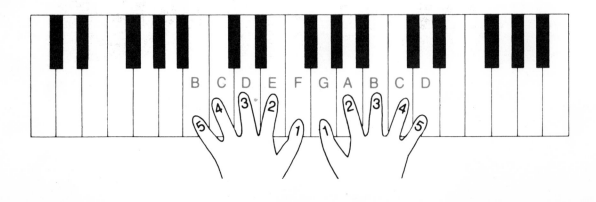

46

JOLLY OLD SAINT NICHOLAS

A A A   A   G G G

Jolly old Saint Nicholas,

                              A

Lean your ear this way.

  F   F   F   F

Don't you tell a single soul

  D   D   D D C C   F

What I'm going to say.

             G   A G

What I'm going to say.

  E F

Christmas Eve is coming soon,

  A A   A A G G

Now you dear old man.

                     A

Whisper what you'll bring to me.

  F   F   F   F

Tell me what you can.

  D D   D   D   C   C F

  G   G   A

Tell me what you can.

  F   F

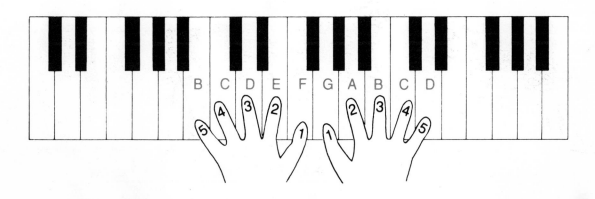

47

WE WISH YOU A MERRY CHRISTMAS

      D

We wish you a Merry Christmas,

G   C   C   CB   A A

      D   D E D

We wish you a Merry Christmas,

A   C   B G

      E   E F ED

We wish you a Merry Christmas,

G   C A

      D

And a Happy New Year!

G G A   B   C

Good tidings to you,

G   C   C   C B

Wherever you are,

B C B   A   G

   D   E D   G

Good tidings for Christmas,

          C   G

      D

And a Happy New Year.

G G .A   B   C

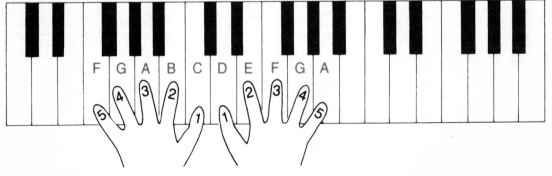

48